Adam Poems - Moments in Verse: A Collection of Life's Experiences, Seen, Felt, and Lived.

Abhijeet Kadam

BookLeaf Publishing

India | USA | UK

Adam Poems - Moments in Verse: A
Collection of Life's Experiences, Seen, Felt,
and Lived. © 2024 Abhijeet Kadam

Presentation by *BookLeaf Publishing*

Web: www.bookleafpub.com

E-mail: info@bookleafpub.com

ISBN:9789363318472

First edition 2024

To Family, Friends, Veera, Veer and Mahadev

PREFACE

Welcome to *Moments in Verse: A Collection of Life's Experiences, Seen, Felt, and Lived.*

In this collection, you will find a series of poems that are deeply personal and profoundly human. They are not the product of careful planning or forced creativity; instead, they are the spontaneous outpourings of emotions, captured in words at the moment when the feeling is strongest.

Each poem in this collection is a reflection of my own experiences, observations, and emotions. They are snapshots of moments in time, frozen in verse, and offered to you with honesty, vulnerability, and love.

Writing these poems has been a deeply personal journey for me, a way to make sense of the world and my place in it. I have written about moments of joy and moments of pain, moments of love and moments of loss. And through it all, I have discovered the power of poetry to heal, to connect, and to illuminate the human experience.

It is my hope that as you read these poems, you will find moments of connection, moments of recognition, and moments of solace. May these words remind you that you are not alone in your experiences and that there is beauty to be found even in the most difficult moments of life.

Thank you for joining me on this journey.

With love,
Abhijeet Kadam

Fallen eyelash

The days are getting longer now,
Yesterday I refused to be in my company,
What happened, when, and how,
For fewer questions the answers are many...

The night has lost its charm,
Unaware of the moment it gets dark,
There is no love, no foul, no harm,
Another answer ends with a question mark...

The morning has no alarm,
A single flavor runs the day,
Reinless horses occupy the farm,
Nothing new to hear, nothing new to say...

The dreams live up to their name,
Simple ambitions turned to prayer,
Days and nights are all the same,
A fallen eyelash is just another strand of hair...

Hiltless sword

The braves have fallen,
The sun is not ready to rise,
If the end kisses you,
It won't be a surprise...

The swords facing the ground,
The shields no longer look round...

The horses have lost their master,
Their lives at stake,
They can't run any faster...

The sons will cry,
The women will weep,
All that glory,
Will vanish in a single sweep...

Someone has to stand,
Stand strong stand tall,
May his people look at him,
May he lead them all...

Lead them to the grave,
Lead them to the shrine,
May they drink the glory,
And carry some for the divine...

Brushstrokes

Close your eyes,
Scribble a dream in the darkness,
Gathering all the self-taught lies,
Perfect those gestured edges...

Darken the borders with haste,
Smudge out what needs to be erased,
Keeping your eyes closed,
Take a moment to retrace...

Rent a few colours,
The darkness is your palette,
Fill the soul with rainbows,
Swirl some red in your goblet...

Let the outline shine,
Some wilderness will try to provoke,
Know you are making a masterpiece,
Make sure you hide the brushstrokes...

Here I Stand

Here I stand,
Traveling through the glorious mountain,
Tumbling over the stagnant land,
Scaling my seasonal skin,
In search of a stable hand...

Here I stand,
With reasons of my own,
Trying to be in command,
Analysing the weight of my shield,
Ignorant of my empty hand...

In an illusional war,
No sword will ever be big enough to fight,
No distance will ever be too far,
No truth will ever be divinely right,
There is but a promise of a scar...

I fight a battle of my own,
For an irrelevant outcome,
Matters I need to atone,
Before my hands get numb,
I may sail or choose to strand,
It's my ship,
And here I stand...

How do I say it right?

How do I say it right?
With a thousand words,
Or rhyming birds,
While holding hands,
Or in the middle of a dance,
How do I say it right...?

Will she take me for my word?
Or applaud for the depth of it,
Will she hear it from her heart?
Or will her mind start playing dirty tricks...?

My wrongs are blurry,
And rights are too bright to see,
Locked are her doors for me,
Could my words wield a key...?

Not everything could be shown,
Not everything could be felt,
I stitched back everything that was torn,
Loan me some words,
I need to say it right...

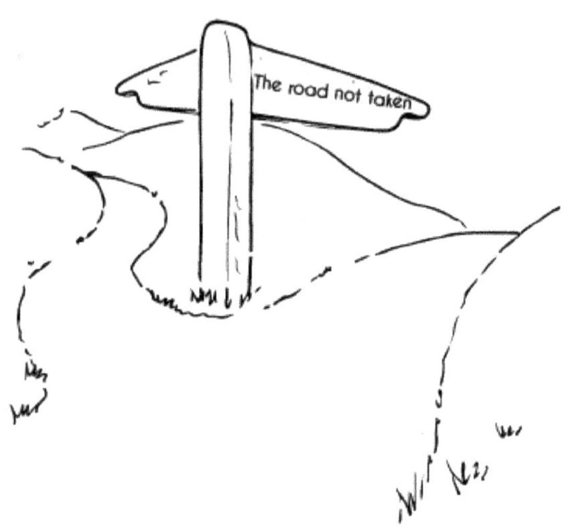
The road not taken

I skipped the Montage

I hear applause –
Cheers rent the air,
And some whistles slide in;
In that blinding light,
I was everything I had never been...

The lights get dimmer
Nudging me from my sleep,
But I still had that smile on me;
Staring into the mirror I set my hair,
I believed I could be anything I wanted to be...

This life feels like my Odyssey;
I've got what I need –
I am being challenged, being pushed
I have been tested, been tempered,
But I know where this long road shall lead…

With that rage, that passion,
I work harder and harder,
At a distance looms my mirage,
I stumble over and over again,
But finally, I built my own montage...

The light is brighter now,
The birds have started to sing,
As I roll my car out of the garage,
And lasso my tie in the rear-view mirror,
I see that I skipped the Montage...

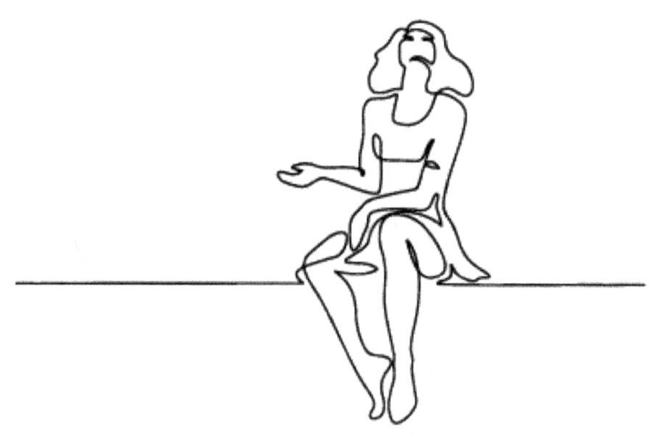

Thousand wrongs

Thousand wrongs did I do,
In search of one right,
What is false and what is true,
Depends on how long you can fight...

Some lies become truth,
Simply by its persistence,
Costs you your entire youth,
To find a reason for your existence...

What wrongs are wrong,
If not done by me, for me,
What wrongs are right,
That prevents me from being free...

A thousand more wrongs will I do,
But to find my own way,
Not sure when the show will find its cue,
But Until then, I shall rehearse the play...

Ashes

One way to look at it,
At life,
It's a collection of memories,
From parents to friends from girlfriends to wife,
It's a collection of stories...

Some start early, some start late,
They swim they dro
wn some merely float,
There is always some chalk left on the slate,
Seldom has it ended on a happy note...

They come back,
They always do,
Manners they surely lack,
With people, I'm talking about memories too...

They bring joy, they bring tear,
Some go far, some come near,
There is always a different story,
But every story has a passage for fear...

Memories do every story cost,
Every story is read with different glasses,
Not everything gone is lost,
Not everything burnt is gone, we still have the
ashes...

Beer's getting cold

I see the glass,
I see the bubbles,
I see the froth,
Diluting all my troubles...
I know the drill,

I know it's wrong,
Hollow emotions I feel,
Singing an untuned song...

Rhythm I do find,
Like a hopeless blind,
My beer's getting cold,
Excuse me, if you don't mind…

Deck of cards

I hold a deck of cards,
Four sets to be precise,
Fifty-two and blacks and reds,
Jokers, I keep them aside...

I collect the clubs and the spades,
And then the diamonds and hearts,
Thirteen they count in their different shades,
Ace and queen remain poles apart...

I put them together with jokers on top,
Just when everything seems to be in place,
The cards make a heavenly drop...

They all fall on the ground,
Some facing me,
Some lying upside-down...

I know I can pick them up,
And arrange them together,
But I stare at the diamond queen,
Waiting for my thoughts to gather...

That moment,
When the cards are scattered,
Twos with kings and Jacks with Jokers,
Some myths are broken, some dreams get
shattered...

Nature's design

The morning sun I got to meet,
On to the heights of amazing feet,
The waters below, massive and blue,
Blessed was I to see them greet...

Placed at the top as a dignitary,
He followed us below,
The rivers and its tributaries,
Were all made to glow...

The conical mountains,
And checkered farms,
Explains the temptations,
To widen thy arms...

How they must have made it,
Perfection in randomness,
I may not believe in his existence,
But sure do in the holiness...

A wish to the crows

I remember when I started to sprout,
And recall the moments I gazed at the Sun,
With a prayer for another day,
With a wish for another chance...

There was but another chance,
And the early crows did arrive,
Laying on the bed full of worms,
For another day, they helped me survive...

Now I have grown with the Sun,
And with the rains, I thrived a few more seasons,
Attached and raw,
I search for a purpose, I find reasons...

I hope I find my reasons,
And that it all adds up to nine,
I have but one prayer and a wish,
To the crows,
To help me detach like a gourd from its vine...

Tell the time

At times,
The time is just right,
Sunlight just enough bright,
When you plan to seize the moment,
The feeble clock turns ignorant...

At times,
A thought is brewing,
And a few more accruing,
When the moment arrives,
Nothing but a broken clock survives...

At times,
Some unshackled courage shows up,
Like a knight's picturesque gallop,
But with its two-and-a-half moves,
The mighty clock disapproves...

At times,
All the moments go berserk,
Not knowing how all the pieces in the
clockwork,
I may lose the ability to rhyme,
But I can still tell the time…

I think this is how it works

I think this is how it works,
You are there until you're not,
You loved until you could not,
Frozen drops they call no rain,
Only losses realize the pain...

The pain has never been real,
The situations never ideal,
Thoughts fail to anneal,
Piecemeal life's an ordeal,
And then there is nothing you feel,
I think this is how it works...

The blossomed is named a flower,
Only passed time gets called an hour,
The truth hides in its shell,
Turning into lies as no one could tell,
With thoughts and thoughts, it irks,
I think this is how it works…

Canvas of life

Sometimes life doesn't understand,
Like tides trying to engulf the land,
Sometimes life takes it too far,
Like trapping sunlight in an empty jar,
Sometimes life makes a real mess,
Delivering the right people to the wrong
address...

Sometimes life tries to make it right,
Giving strength to lose another fight,
Sometimes it just doesn't care,
Making everything else look unfair,
Sometimes,
Sometimes it just lets you be,
Testing if it can set you free...

To all the refracting experiences,
The colors life decided to give,
Yes, the canvas is painted,
Got too many brushstrokes to forgive...

Dotted line

A few schools you attended,
To learn all the letters,
It's important they said,
Passing a grade is all that matters...

The colleges thereafter,
Paying a ransom for a paper,
Soul devoid of a rafter,
Did youth do a little caper...?

What about dreams?
The real ones,
Some plausible, some extremes,
Some fights with bullet-less guns...

When there's nothing to design,
Thoughts, no longer divine,
In that moment and time,
They make you sign,
On a dotted line...

Don't disturb the silence

Leaning against a rock,
The stars were gazing at me stare,
A chaotic ripple ran through the lake,
A star loosened up to start a lovely affair...

A few more stars joined the party,
The breeze brought a moment of dalliance,
Heart filled with some cold air,
I decided not to disturb the silence...

A cricket joined the romance,
The moon was nowhere to be seen,
The ripple now touched the shore,
And the silence uttered amen…

The stupid poem

I am sitting on a couch, that is red and brown,
I am feeling like a king, just without a crown,
The clock's ticking, tick-tock, in its way,
I am sitting idle, I've nothing to say,
I am writing this poem in a stupid way...

The doors are closed and the windows shut,
The floor is dirty and covered with dust,
My hands are dirty and so are my feet,
I am hungry, oh baby, I need something to eat,
I got nothing to do, I got nothing to say,
I am writing this poem in a stupider way...

The sun's gone down and it's very dark,
My TV shows a ship and a big white shark,
It's time for dinner and I am on my way,
I am going to a hotel, I need cash to pay,
I've written this poem in the stupidest way...

Sorry to waste your time...

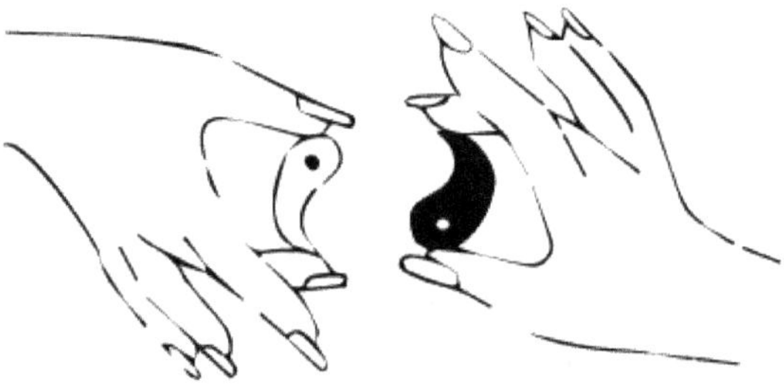

Glory rainbow

From the glory rainbow,
Pluck the colour blue,
Carry it for the one to show,
With some dreams and a few wishes too...

Farewell thoughts are distant,
Today we do not bid adieu,
Now that the sky is consistent,
A few more wishes are definitely due...

All the secrets you want to share,
And the thoughts you want to feel,
In those moments of despair,
A wish is all you dream to steal...

Some dreams need to grow,
For what you want it to be,
What you see and what you show,
It's time they both agree…

Broken halo

And today, after yesterday,
I feel good,
I said what I wanted to say,
Now I don't have to pay,
Do you...?

Wait for,
When the day's right,
And a bright night,
When you lose the fight,
With you...

The fights are many not one,
Remember from where you come,
Acknowledge what you become,
A good daughter or a good son,
Will you...?

It's just a matter of time,
Half a life is pending alive,
Now you know how to revive,
Now you know how to survive,
Broken halo but an angel can fly,
For you...

So today, after yesterday,
Shout 'I feel good',
After a lengthy essay,
Let it drift further away,
You said what you wanted to say,
Didn't you...?

After all,
It's just a matter of time,
Half-life is pending alive,
Now you know how to revive,
Now you know how to survive,
Broken halo but an angel can fly,
For you...

Tired promise

The journey is now off the road,
The wind and the breath both getting cold,
At a distance lies the mountain,
The tale of which has never been told...

Now the bones have felt the shiver,
Wishing some warmth for the beating heart,
High up north flows a frozen river,
The tale finds words to describe the start...

Tired and weary now feels the sole,
Frayed laces gather some strength to hold,
Black is the sky from pole to pole,
Alive with a promise of the tale to be told…